Greatest Ever

Baking

The All Time Top 20 Greatest Recipes

Greatest Ever

Baking

The All Time Top 20 Greatest Recipes

p

NOTE

This book uses metric and imperial measurements. Follow the same
units of measurement throughout; do not mix metric and imperial.
All spoon measurements are level: teaspoons are assumed to be 5 ml,
and tablespoons are assumed to be 15 ml. Unless otherwise stated,
milk is assumed to be whole milk, eggs and individual vegetables such as
potatoes are medium, and pepper is freshly ground black pepper.

The times given for each recipe are an approximate guide only because the
preparation times may differ according to the techniques used by different
people and the cooking times may vary as a result of the type of oven used.
The preparation times include chilling times, where appropriate.

Recipes using raw or very lightly cooked eggs should be
avoided by infants, the elderly, pregnant women, convalescents,
and anyone suffering from an illness.

C O N T E N T S

6   INTRODUCTION

12   SANDWICH CAKE WITH CHOCOLATE TOPPING

13   SPICED BREAD & BUTTER PUDDING

14   CLASSIC CARROT CAKE

15   LEMON SPONGE CAKE

16   GOLDEN FRUIT CAKE

17   SPICY FRUIT LOAF

18   CRANBERRY & ALMOND TART

19   SULTANA & CHERRY SCONES

20   MINI MERINGUES

21   MIXED FRUIT PAVLOVA

22   SPICED APPLE GINGERBREAD

23   MIXED FRUIT CRUMBLE

24   LEMON CREAM BUTTERFLIES

25   CHOCOLATE & PEAR SPONGE

26   BUTTERY LEMON FLAN

27   TREACLE SCONES

28   BAKED APPLE & SULTANA PUDDING

29   RASPBERRY & CREAM SHORTBREAD

30   BERRY CHEESECAKE

31   STRAWBERRY ROULADE

32   INDEX

INTRODUCTIO

Baking is an incredibly satisfying activity. You start with a few shapeless ingredients – flour, sugar, fat and eggs – and turn them into beautiful mouthwatering cakes, biscuits, pies, breads and desserts to delight your family and friends.

In just 20 recipes, you are introduced to all the skills of baking and discover how to create some of the best-loved cakes, biscuits, scones and flans. Clear, step-by-step instructions guide you through the techniques needed to mastermind all those baking favourites that have been savoured and enjoyed from generation to generation.

CAKE-BAKING AND STORAGE

Do not be too impatient and open the oven door while your cake is baking. Wait until it has nearly finished cooking before testing to see if it is ready. When cooked, the cake will have shrunk away from the sides of the tin slightly. Press the centre of the top lightly with your fingertips – it should spring back at once. Alternatively, push a fine metal skewer into the centre of the cake – if it comes out clean, the cake is done.

Leave the cake in its tin to cool slightly before turning out on to a wire rack to cool completely. Store the finished cake in an airtight container.

Above: The dried ingredients used in cake-baking should be measured out very carefully. Use good quality, fresh ingredients to achieve the best results.

FAMILY FAVOURITES

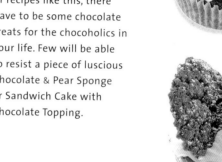

So what's to stop you baking your way into your family's good books and impressing your friends? Even mundane coffee breaks and children's packed lunches will be much more popular with the offer of a piece of home-baked Golden Fruit Cake or some delicious Treacle Scones to go with them.

The tasty Spiced Apple Gingerbread and Classic Carrot Cake are more down-to-earth, cut-and-come-again treats to keep in the cake tin – if you can – to satisfy an attack of the munchies.

The Sultana & Cherry Scones and Spicy Fruit Loaf are comfortingly familiar and excellent served with morning coffee or afternoon tea. If you are new to baking you'll be pleasantly surprised by how straightforward they are to make.

Even in a small selection of recipes like this, there have to be some chocolate treats for the chocoholics in your life. Few will be able to resist a piece of luscious Chocolate & Pear Sponge or Sandwich Cake with Chocolate Topping.

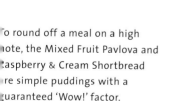

To round off a meal on a high note, the Mixed Fruit Pavlova and Raspberry & Cream Shortbread are simple puddings with a guaranteed 'Wow!' factor.

7

GOLDEN RULES OF BAKIN

scales

box grater

Making cakes

Clear, step-by-step instructions guide you through the measuring, mixing and baking of each recipe. Baking calls for precision and there are some ground rules you should always follow:

★ Make sure you read the recipe from start to finish so you know what ingredients and cake tins you need.

★ Weigh out all the ingredients accurately and do any preparation, such as grating, chopping or tin greasing and lining, before you start mixing.

★ Keep cake ingredients at room temperature.

★ Mix thoroughly, with the firmness or delicacy recommended, and for as long as the recipe requires.

★ Use a metal spoon or plastic spatula for folding flour into cake mixtures, sugar into whisked egg whites or egg whites into the rest of the ingredients

★ Always use the size and shape of tin recommended in the recipe, otherwise the cake may not cook properly in the time allowed.

Making pastry for tarts

When making pastry for the flans and tarts in this book, follow this basic method:

1 Sift the dry ingredients into a large mixing bowl, add the diced fat and toss it through the flour.

2 Gently rub the fat between your fingertips, until the mixture resembles fine breadcrumbs. To make light pastry, raise your hands as you rub the fat into the flour to aerate the mixture as it falls back into the bowl.

measuring spoons

Left: A set of measuring spoons ensures accurate and consistent measurements

pecan nuts

Lightly bind the mixture with iced water or other specified liquid, using just enough to form the crumbs into a ball of soft but not sticky dough. Wrap the dough in clingfilm and chill for at least 30 minutes before rolling out.

dark chocolate

Using chocolate

Bittersweet, dark chocolate is most popular for baking. Dark chocolate with between 50 and 72 per cent cocoa solids is suitable for everyday cooking.

Break the chocolate into small, equal-sized pieces and put them in a heatproof bowl. Sit the bowl over a pan of simmering water, with its base clear of the water. As the chocolate starts to melt, stir gently until smooth. Make sure that no water splashes into the molten chocolate or it will solidify.

To melt the chocolate in a microwave, place small pieces in a microwave-proof bowl. Timing varies according to the type and quantity of chocolate. As a guide, 125 g/4½ oz dark chocolate takes 2 minutes on High to melt; white or milk chocolate takes 2–3 minutes on Medium.

When the time is up, stir the chocolate and leave to stand for a few minutes before stirring again. If necessary return the bowl to the microwave for a further 30 seconds.

Setting chocolate

Chocolate sets best at 18°C/65°F, although it will set more slowly in a slightly warmer room. If set in the refrigerator it may develop a white bloom and be very brittle. If possible, set chocolate decorations in a cool room.

eggs

oranges

Right: Melted chocolate solidifies into a mouthwatering cake topping.

Before you start baking any of the cakes, scones, flans or breads in this book you will need to check that you have some basic equipment.

spatula

wooden spoon

EQUIPMENT

mixing bowl

basin

ramekin dishes

Scales

As the precise measurement of ingredients is important in baking, it is hard to manage without scales. Make sure that the dial or display is clear enough to read easily.

Measuring jug

This is handy for measuring an exact quantity of liquid. A 1.2-litre/2-pint size is the most useful.

Measuring spoons

A full set of measuring spoons usually includes a ¼ teaspoon, ½ teaspoon, 1 teaspoon and 1 tablespoon. They are useful for measuring small amounts of raising agents and spices.

Sieve

It is a good idea to keep a separate sieve for sifting dry ingredients, such as flour and icing sugar, to remove the lumps and add air.

Mixing bowl

A large, rounded stainless steel, glass, plastic or glazed ceramic bowl is invaluable for mixing ingredients.

Basins

You will need several smaller basins for beating eggs or whipping cream, and for assembling ingredients before mixing.

Wooden spoons

A large, flat, wooden spoon is good for creaming butter and sugar together.

astic spatulas

ese are used for folding in
gredients and for scraping
ut the last remnants of the
ixture from the bowl.

ake tins

ways buy the best quality
ns you can afford: non-stick
rfaces are helpful but still
quire a light coating of oil.
ake sure you wash and dry
e tins well before storing.
heck the recipe first to find
ut what shape and size of
ke or loaf tin you need.

an tins

metal flan tin cooks the
astry more crisply than
lass or ceramic dishes.
oose-based tins with
movable sides are the best.
20-cm/8-inch flan tin is the
ost useful size.

Baking sheets and trays

A good heavyweight baking
sheet and tray are essential
because they will not buckle
in the oven.

Cooling rack

A cooling rack allows the
steam to escape from a baked
item and prevents it from
becoming soggy.

Rolling pin

To roll pastry well you need a
heavy, smooth rolling pin. In
emergencies a milk bottle
will do but it does not give an
even rolling.

Palette knife

This long-bladed, flexible
knife is used for spreading
whipped cream and icing.

Pastry brush

A brush is useful for dusting
excess flour from pastry,
applying an egg or milk glaze
or greasing tins. Make sure
you wash and dry the brush
well, or the bristles will start
to fall out.

Pastry cutters

These are available in a range
of shapes and sizes, fluted
and plain, and are used for
stamping out scones and
biscuits. Make sure you wash
and dry them well after use
to prevent them rusting.

baking trays

food mixer

pastry brushes

pastry cutters

SANDWICH CAKE WITH CHOCOLATE TOPPING

>Serves 8–10   >Preparation time: 1 hour   >Cooking time: 20 minutes

INGREDIENTS

125 g/4½ oz soft margarine

125 g/4½ oz caster sugar

2 eggs

1 tbsp golden syrup

125 g/4½ oz self-raising flour, sieved

2 tbsp cocoa powder, sieved

FILLING AND TOPPING

50 g/1¾ oz icing sugar, sieved

2 tbsp butter

100 g/3½ oz white or milk cooking chocolate

a little milk or white chocolate, melted (optional)

METHOD

1 Lightly grease two 18-cm/7-inch shallow cake tins.

2 Place all of the cake ingredients in a large mixing bowl and beat with a wooden spoon electric hand whisk to form a smooth mixtur

3 Divide the mixture between the prepared tins and level the tops. Bake the cake layers i a preheated oven, 190°C/375°F/Gas Mark 5, for 20 minutes, or until springy to the touch. Cool for a few minutes in the tins before transferring to a wire rack to cool completely

4 To make the filling, beat the icing sugar an butter together in a bowl until light and fluff Melt the cooking chocolate and beat half into the icing mixture. Use the filling to sandwich the 2 cakes together.

5 Spread the remaining melted cooking chocolate over the top of the cake. Pipe circle of melted milk or white chocolate, if using, a feather into the cooking chocolate with a cocktail stick. Leave to set before serving.

PICED BREAD & UTTER PUDDING

erves 6 ➤Preparation time: 1 hour ➤Cooking time: 40–45 minutes

GREDIENTS

o g/7 oz white bread, sliced

tbsp butter, softened

g/1 oz sultanas

g/1 oz mixed peel

tsp ground mixed spice

JSTARD

›o ml/1 pint milk

egg yolks

g/2¾ oz caster sugar

ETHOD

Grease a 1.2-litre/2-pint ovenproof dish.

Remove the crusts from the bread, if liked, read with butter and cut into quarters.

Arrange half of the buttered bread slices in e prepared ovenproof dish. Sprinkle half of e sultanas and mixed peel over the top of e bread.

4 Place the remaining bread slices over the fruit, then sprinkle over the reserved fruit.

5 To make the custard, bring the milk almost to the boil in a saucepan. Whisk together the egg yolks and the sugar in a bowl, then pour in the warm milk.

6 Strain the warm custard through a sieve. Pour the custard over the bread slices.

7 Leave to stand for 30 minutes, then sprinkle with the ground mixed spice.

8 Place the ovenproof dish in a roasting tin half-filled with hot water.

9 Bake in a preheated oven, 200°C/400°F/Gas Mark 6, for 40–45 minutes, or until the pudding has just set. Serve warm.

CLASSIC CARROT CAKE

> Makes 12 bars > Preparation time: 10 minutes > Cooking time: 20–25 minutes

INGREDIENTS

125 g/4½ oz self-raising flour

pinch of salt

1 tsp ground cinnamon

125 g/4½ oz soft brown sugar

2 eggs

100 ml/3½ fl oz sunflower oil

125 g/4½ oz carrot, peeled and finely grated

25 g/1 oz desiccated coconut

25 g/1 oz walnuts, chopped

walnut pieces, for decoration

ICING

4 tbsp butter, softened

50 g/1¼ oz full-fat soft cheese

225 g/8 oz icing sugar, sieved

1 tsp lemon juice

METHOD

1 Lightly grease a 20-cm/8-inch square cake t
and line with baking paper.

2 Sieve the flour, salt and ground cinnamon
into a large bowl and stir in the brown sugar
Add the eggs and oil to the dry ingredients a
mix well.

3 Stir in the grated carrot, desiccated coconu
and chopped walnuts.

4 Pour the mixture into the prepared tin and
bake in a preheated oven, 180°C/350°F/Gas
Mark 4, for 20–25 minutes, or until just firm
the touch. Leave to cool in the tin.

5 Meanwhile, make the icing. In a bowl, beat
together the butter, full-fat soft cheese, icing
sugar and lemon juice until the mixture is
fluffy and creamy.

6 Turn the cake out of the tin, spread with th
icing, and cut into 12 bars or slices. Decorate
with walnut pieces.

EMON SPONGE CAKE

erves 8 ➤Preparation time: 1 hour ➤Cooking time: 45 minutes–1 hour

INGREDIENTS

o g/7 oz plain flour

sp baking powder

o g/7 oz caster sugar

eggs

o ml/5 fl oz soured cream

ated rind 1 large lemon

tbsp lemon juice

o ml/5 fl oz sunflower oil

RUP

tbsp icing sugar

tbsp lemon juice

ETHOD

ightly grease a 20-cm/8-inch loose-
ttomed round cake tin and line the base
th baking paper.

Sieve the flour and baking powder into a
ixing bowl and stir in the caster sugar.

3 In a separate mixing bowl, whisk the eggs,
soured cream, lemon rind, lemon juice and
sunflower oil together.

4 Pour the egg mixture into the dry ingredients
and mix well until evenly combined.

5 Pour the mixture into the prepared tin and
bake in a preheated oven, 180°C/350°F/Gas
Mark 4, for 45–60 minutes until risen and
golden brown.

6 Meanwhile, to make the syrup, mix together
the icing sugar and lemon juice in a small
saucepan. Stir over a low heat until just
beginning to bubble and turn syrupy.

7 As soon as the cake comes out of the oven,
prick the surface with a fine skewer, then
brush the syrup over the top. Leave the cake to
cool completely in the tin before turning out
and serving.

GOLDEN FRUIT CAKE

>Serves 8–10   >Preparation time: 1 hour   >Cooking time: 1 hour

INGREDIENTS

100 g/3½ oz butter, softened

100g/3½ oz caster sugar

2 eggs, beaten

50 g/1¼ oz self-raising flour, sieved

100 g/3½ oz polenta

1 tsp baking powder

225 g/8 oz mixed dried fruit

25 g/1 oz pine kernels

grated rind of 1 lemon

4 tbsp lemon juice

2 tbsp milk

METHOD

1 Grease an 18-cm/7-inch cake tin and line the base with baking paper.

2 In a bowl, whisk together the butter and sugar until light and fluffy.

3 Whisk in the beaten eggs a little at a time, whisking well after each addition.

4 Fold the flour, polenta and baking powder into the mixture until well blended.

5 Stir in the mixed dried fruit, pine kernels, grated lemon rind, lemon juice and milk.

6 Spoon the mixture into the prepared tin and level the surface.

7 Bake in a preheated oven, 180°C/350°F/Gas Mark 4, for 1 hour, or until a skewer inserted into the centre of the cake comes out clean.

8 Leave the cake to cool in the tin before turning out.

PICY FRUIT LOAF

akes a 900 g/2 lb loaf ❯Preparation time: 1 hour ❯Cooking time: 1–1¼ hours

GREDIENTS

g/12 oz plain flour

ch of salt

sp baking powder

sp ground cinnamon

g/5½ oz butter, cut into small pieces

g/4½ oz soft brown sugar

g/6 oz currants

ely grated rind of 1 orange

tbsp orange juice

sp milk

ggs, lightly beaten

THOD

rease a 900-g/2-lb loaf tin and line the base
oothly with baking paper.

2 Sieve the flour, salt, baking powder and
ground cinnamon into a bowl. Then rub in the
pieces of butter with your fingers, until the
mixture resembles coarse breadcrumbs.

3 Stir in the sugar, currants and orange rind.
Beat the orange juice, milk and eggs together
and add to the dry ingredients. Mix well
together.

4 Spoon the mixture into the prepared tin.
Make a slight dip in the middle of the mixture
to help it rise evenly.

5 Bake in a preheated oven, 180°C/350°F/Gas
Mark 4, for about 1–1¼ hours, or until a fine
metal skewer inserted into the centre of the
loaf comes out clean.

6 Leave the loaf to cool before turning out of
the tin. Transfer to a wire rack and leave to cool
completely before slicing.

CRANBERRY & ALMOND TAR

>Serves 8–10   >Preparation time: 1½ hours   >Cooking time: 1½ hours

INGREDIENTS

PASTRY

150 g/5½ oz plain flour

125 g/4½ oz caster sugar

125 g/4½ oz butter, cut into small pieces

1 tbsp water

FILLING

200 g/7 oz unsalted butter

200g/7 oz caster sugar

1 egg

2 egg yolks

40 g/1½ oz plain flour, sieved

175 g/6 oz ground almonds

4 tbsp double cream

410 g/14½ oz canned apricot halves, drained

125 g/4½ oz fresh cranberries

METHOD

1 To make the pastry, place the flour and sugar in a bowl and rub in the butter with your fingers. Add the water and work the mixture together until a soft dough has formed. Wrap and chill for 30 minutes.

2 On a lightly floured surface, roll out the dough and line a 24-cm/9½-inch loose-bottomed flan tin. Prick the pastry with a fo and chill for 30 minutes.

3 Line the pastry case with foil and baking beans and bake in a preheated oven, 190°C/375°F/Gas Mark 5, for 15 minutes. Remove the foil and baking beans and cook a further 10 minutes.

4 To make the filling, cream together the butter and sugar until light and fluffy. Beat i the egg and egg yolks, then stir in the flour, almonds and cream.

5 Place the apricot halves and cranberries on the bottom of the pastry case and spoon the filling over the top.

6 Bake in the oven for about 1 hour, or until t topping is just set. Leave to cool slightly, the serve warm or cold.

ULTANA & CHERRY SCONES

Makes 8 ➤ Preparation time: 30 minutes ➤ Cooking time: 8–10 minutes

GREDIENTS

5 g/8 oz self-raising flour

bsp caster sugar

nch of salt

g/2¾ oz butter, cut into small pieces

g/1½ oz glacé cherries, chopped

g/1½ oz sultanas

gg, beaten

bsp milk

ETHOD

ightly grease a baking tray.

ieve the flour, sugar and salt into a mixing
wl and rub in the butter with your fingers
til the mixture resembles breadcrumbs.

tir in the glacé cherries and sultanas. Add
e egg.

4 Reserve 1 tablespoon of the milk for glazing,
then add the remainder to the mixture. Mix
together to form a soft dough.

5 On a lightly floured surface, roll out the
dough to a thickness of 2 cm/¾ inch and cut
out 8 scones, using a 5-cm/2-inch cutter.

6 Place the scones on to the baking tray and
brush with the reserved milk.

7 Bake in a preheated oven, 220°C/425°F/Gas
Mark 7, for 8–10 minutes, or until the scones
are golden brown.

8 Leave to cool on a wire rack, then serve split
in half spread with butter.

MINI MERINGUES

> Makes about 13   > Preparation time: 20 minutes   > Cooking time: 1½ hours

INGREDIENTS

4 egg whites

pinch of salt

125 g/4½ oz granulated sugar

125 g/4½ oz caster sugar

300 ml/10 fl oz double cream, lightly whipped

METHOD

1 Line 3 baking trays with baking paper.

2 In a large, clean bowl, whisk together the egg whites and salt until they are stiff, using an electric hand-held whisk or a balloon whisk. (You should be able to turn the bowl upside down without any movement from the whisked egg whites.)

3 Whisk in the granulated sugar a little at a time; at this stage, the meringue should start to look glossy.

4 Sprinkle in the caster sugar a little at a time and continue whisking until all the sugar has been incorporated and the meringue is thick, white and stands in tall peaks.

5 Transfer the meringue mixture to a piping bag fitted with a 2-cm/¾-inch star nozzle. Pipe about 26 small whirls on to the prepared baking trays.

6 Bake in a preheated oven, 120°C/250°F/Gas Mark ½, for 1½ hours, or until the meringues are pale golden in colour and can be easily lifted off the paper. Leave them to cool in the turned-off oven overnight.

7 Just before serving, sandwich the meringues together in pairs with the cream and arrange on a serving plate.

MIXED FRUIT PAVLOVA

>Serves 6   >Preparation time: 1¼ hours   >Cooking time: 1¼ hours

INGREDIENTS

3 egg whites

pinch of salt

175 g/6 oz caster sugar

300 ml/10 fl oz double cream, lightly whipped

fresh fruit of your choice, such as raspberries, strawberries, peaches, passion fruit and cape gooseberries

METHOD

1 Line a baking sheet with baking paper.

2 Whisk the egg whites with the salt in a large bowl until they form soft peaks.

3 Whisk in the sugar a little at a time, whisking well after each addition until all of the sugar has been incorporated.

4 Spoon three-quarters of the meringue on to the baking sheet, forming a round 20 cm/ 8 inches in diameter.

5 Place spoonfuls of the remaining meringue all around the edge of the round so they join up to make a nest shape.

6 Bake in a preheated oven, 140°C/275°F/Gas Mark 1, for 1¼ hours.

7 Turn the heat off, but leave the pavlova in the oven until completely cold.

8 Place the pavlova on a serving dish. Spread with the lightly whipped cream, then arrange the fresh fruit on top.

SPICED APPLE GINGERBREAD

>Makes 12 bars   >Preparation time: 1¼ hours   >Cooking time: 30–35 minutes

INGREDIENTS

150 g/5½ oz butter

175 g/6 oz soft brown sugar

2 tbsp black treacle

225 g/8 oz plain flour

1 tsp baking powder

2 tsp bicarbonate of soda

2 tsp ground ginger

150 ml/5 fl oz milk

1 egg, beaten

2 dessert apples, peeled, chopped and coated with 1 tbsp lemon juice

METHOD

1 Grease a 23-cm/9-inch square cake tin and line with baking paper.

2 Melt the butter, sugar and treacle in a saucepan over a low heat and leave the mixture to cool.

3 Sieve the flour, baking powder, bicarbonate of soda and ginger into a mixing bowl.

4 Stir in the milk, beaten egg and cooled buttery liquid, followed by the chopped apples coated with the lemon juice.

5 Mix everything together gently, then pour the mixture into the prepared tin.

6 Bake in a preheated oven, 160°C/325°F/Gas Mark 3, for 30–35 minutes, or until the cake has risen and a fine skewer inserted into the centre comes out clean.

7 Leave the cake to cool in the tin before turning out and cutting into 12 bars.

MIXED FRUIT CRUMBLE

>Serves 4 >Preparation time: 10 minutes >Cooking time: 50 minutes

INGREDIENTS

2 mangoes, sliced

1 pawpaw, seeded and sliced

225 g/8 oz fresh pineapple, cubed

1½ tsp ground ginger

100 g/3½ oz margarine

100 g/3½ oz light brown sugar

175 g/6 oz plain flour

50 g/1¼ oz desiccated coconut, plus extra
to decorate

METHOD

1 Place the fruit in a pan with ½ tsp of the ginger, 30 g/1 oz of the margarine and 50 g/1¼ oz of the sugar. Cook over a low heat for 10 minutes, until the fruit softens. Spoon the fruit into the base of a shallow ovenproof dish.

2 Mix the flour and remaining ginger together. Rub in the remaining margarine until the mixture resembles fine breadcrumbs. Stir in the remaining sugar and the coconut and spoon over the fruit to cover completely.

3 Cook the crumble in a preheated oven, 180°C/350°F/Gas Mark 4, for about 40 minutes, or until the top is crisp. Decorate with a sprinkling of desiccated coconut and serve.

LEMON CREAM BUTTERFLIE

> Makes 12   > Preparation time: 30 minutes   > Cooking time: 15 minutes

INGREDIENTS

125 g/4½ oz soft margarine

125 g/4½ oz caster sugar

150 g/5½ oz self-raising flour

2 large eggs

2 tbsp cocoa powder

25 g/1 oz dark chocolate, melted

icing sugar, to dust

LEMON BUTTER CREAM

100 g/3½ oz unsalted butter, softened

225 g/8 oz icing sugar, sieved

grated rind of ½ lemon

1 tbsp lemon juice

METHOD

1 Place 12 paper cases in a muffin pan. Place all of the ingredients for the cakes, except for the melted chocolate, in a large mixing bowl and beat with electric beaters until the mixture is just smooth. Beat in the chocolate.

2 Spoon equal amounts of the cake mixture into each paper case, filling them three-quarters full. Bake in a preheated oven, 180°C/350°F/Gas Mark 4, for 15 minutes, or un springy to the touch. Transfer the cakes to a wire rack and leave to cool.

3 To make the lemon butter cream, place the butter in a mixing bowl and beat until fluffy, then gradually beat in the icing sugar. Beat in the lemon rind and gradually add the lem juice, beating well.

4 When cold, cut the top off each cake, using serrated knife. Cut each top in half.

5 Spread or pipe the butter cream icing over the cut surface of each cake and push the 2 c pieces of cake top into the icing to form wing Sprinkle with icing sugar.

CHOCOLATE & PEAR SPONGE

Serves 6 ➤ Preparation time: 1¼ hours ➤ Cooking time: 1 hour

INGREDIENTS

175 g/6 oz butter, softened

175 g/6 oz soft brown sugar

3 eggs, beaten

150 g/5½ oz self-raising flour

1 tbsp cocoa powder

1 tbsp milk

3 small pears, peel, cored and sliced

METHOD

1 Grease a 23-cm/8-inch loose-bottomed cake tin and line the base with baking parchment.

2 In a bowl, cream together the butter and soft brown sugar until pale and fluffy.

3 Gradually add the beaten eggs to the mixture, beating well after each addition.

4 Sieve the self-raising flour and cocoa powder into the creamed mixture and fold in gently until all of the ingredients are combined.

5 Stir in the milk, then spoon the mixture into the prepared tin. Level the surface with the back of a spoon or a knife.

6 Arrange the pear slices on top of the sponge mixture in a radiating pattern.

7 Bake in a preheated oven, 180°C/350°F/Gas Mark 4, for about 1 hour, or until the sponge is just firm to the touch.

8 Leave the sponge to cool in the tin, then transfer to a wire rack to cool completely before serving.

BUTTERY LEMON FLAN

>Serves 8 >Preparation time: 1½ hours >Cooking time: 50 minutes

INGREDIENTS

PASTRY

150 g/5½ oz plain flour

25 g/1 oz caster sugar

125 g/4½ oz butter, cut into small pieces

1 tbsp water

icing sugar, for dusting

FILLING

150 ml/5 fl oz double cream

100 g/3½ oz caster sugar

4 eggs

grated rind of 3 lemons

12 tbsp lemon juice

METHOD

1 To make the pastry, place the flour and sugar in a bowl and rub in the butter using your fingers. Add the water and mix until a soft dough has formed. Wrap the dough and chill for 30 minutes.

2 On a lightly floured surface, roll out the dough and line a 24-cm/9½-inch loose-bottomed flan tin. Prick the pastry with a fork and chill for 30 minutes.

3 Line the pastry case with foil and baking beans and bake in a preheated oven, 190°C/375°F/Gas Mark 5, for 15 minutes. Remove the foil and baking beans and cook for a further 15 minutes.

4 To make the filling, whisk the cream, sugar, eggs, lemon rind and juice together. Place the pastry case, still in its tin, on a baking tray and pour in the filling.

5 Bake in the oven for about 20 minutes, or until just set. Leave to cool, then lightly dust with icing sugar before serving.

REACLE SCONES

Serves 8 ▸Preparation time: 15 minutes ▸Cooking time: 8–10 minutes

INGREDIENTS

25 g/8 oz self-raising flour

1 tbsp caster sugar

pinch of salt

1 tbsp butter, chilled and cut into small pieces

1 dessert apple, peeled, cored and chopped

1 egg, beaten

1 tbsp black treacle

1 tbsp milk

METHOD

1 Lightly grease a baking tray with butter.

2 Sieve the flour, sugar and salt into a bowl.

3 Add the butter and rub it in with your fingertips until the mixture resembles fine breadcrumbs.

4 Stir the chopped apple into the mixture until thoroughly combined.

5 Mix the beaten egg, treacle and milk together in a jug. Add the mixture to the dry ingredients and mix well to form a soft dough.

6 On a lightly floured work surface, roll out the dough to a thickness of 2 cm/³⁄₄ inch. Cut out 8 scones, using a 5-cm/2-inch cutter.

7 Arrange the treacle scones on the prepared baking tray and bake in a preheated oven, 220°C/425°F/Gas Mark 7, for 8–10 minutes.

8 Transfer the scones to a wire rack and leave to cool slightly. Serve split in half and spread with butter.

BAKED APPLE & SULTANA PUDDING

>Serves 6   >Preparation time: 15 minutes   >Cooking time: 40–45 minutes

INGREDIENTS

450 g/1 lb cooking apples, peeled, cored
and sliced

75 g/2¾ oz granulated sugar

1 tbsp lemon juice

50 g/1¾ oz sultanas

75 g/2¾ oz butter

75 g/2¾ oz caster sugar

1 egg, beaten

150 g/5½ oz self-raising flour

3 tbsp milk

25 g/1 oz flaked almonds

custard or double cream, to serve

METHOD

1 Grease an 850-ml/1½-pint ovenproof dish.

2 Mix the apples with the sugar, lemon juice
and sultanas. Spoon the mixture into the
greased dish.

3 In a mixing bowl, cream the butter and
caster sugar together until pale. Add the egg
a little at a time.

4 Carefully fold in the self-raising flour and st
in the milk, which should give the mixture a
soft, dropping consistency.

5 Spread the mixture over the apples and
sprinkle with the flaked almonds.

6 Bake in a preheated oven, 180°C/350°F/Gas
Mark 4, for 40–45 minutes, or until the spong
is golden brown.

7 Serve the pudding piping hot, accompanied
by custard or double cream

ASPBERRY & CREAM SHORTBREAD

Serves 8   ❯Preparation time: 40 minutes   ❯Cooking time: 15 minutes

INGREDIENTS

175 g/6 oz self-raising flour

100 g/3½ oz butter, cut into cubes

65 g/2¼ oz caster sugar

1 egg yolk

1 tbsp rose water

600 ml/1 pint whipping cream, lightly whipped

225 g/8 oz raspberries, plus a few
for decoration

TO DECORATE

icing sugar

METHOD

1 Lightly grease 2 baking sheets.

2 To make the shortbreads, sieve the flour into a mixing bowl. Rub the butter into the flour with your fingers until the mixture resembles breadcrumbs.

3 Stir the sugar, egg yolk and rose water into the mixture and bring together with your fingers to form a soft dough. Divide the dough in half.

4 Roll each piece of dough to a 20-cm/8-inch round and lift each one on to a prepared baking sheet. Crimp the edges of the dough.

5 Bake in a preheated oven, 190°C/375°F/Gas Mark 5, for 15 minutes, or until lightly golden. Transfer the shortcakes to a wire rack and leave to cool.

6 Mix the cream with the raspberries and spoon on top of one of the shortbreads. Top with the other shortbread round, dust with a little icing sugar and decorate with the extra raspberries you kept back.

BERRY CHEESECAKE

❯Serves 8   ❯Preparation time: 2½ hours   ❯Cooking time: 5 minutes

INGREDIENTS

BASE

75 g/2¾ oz margarine

175 g/6 oz oatmeal biscuits

50 g/1¾ oz desiccated coconut

FILLING

9 tbsp cold water

1½ tsp vegetarian gelatine

125 ml/4 fl oz evaporated milk

1 egg

75 g/2¾ oz soft light brown sugar

450 g/1 lb soft cream cheese

350 g/12 oz mixed berries

2 tbsp clear honey, for drizzling

METHOD

1 Place the margarine in a saucepan and heat until melted. Put the biscuits in a food processor and process until thoroughly crushed. Alternatively, crush finely with a rolling pin. Stir the biscuit crumbs into the margarine, together with the coconut.

2 Lightly grease a 20-cm/8-inch springform tin and line the base with baking parchment. Press the biscuit mixture evenly into the tin. Set aside in the refrigerator to chill while you prepare the filling for the cheesecake.

3 To make the filling, put the water in a pan and sprinkle the gelatine into it. Stir to dissolve. Bring to the boil and boil for 2 minutes. Leave to cool slightly.

4 Put the milk, egg, sugar and soft cream cheese in a bowl and beat until smooth. Stir in 50 g/1¾ oz of the berries. Add the gelatine in a stream, stirring constantly.

5 Spread the mixture on the biscuit base and return to the refrigerator to chill for 2 hours, or until set.

6 Remove the berry cheesecake from the tin and transfer it to a large serving plate. Arrange the remaining berries on top of the cheesecake, drizzle the honey over the top and serve.

TRAWBERRY ROULADE

Serves 8 ▸Preparation time: 45 minutes ▸Cooking time: 8–10 minutes

INGREDIENTS

large eggs

5 g/4¼ oz caster sugar

5 g/4¼ oz plain flour

tbsp hot water

FILLING

00 ml/7 fl oz low-fat fromage frais

tsp almond essence

25 g/8 oz small strawberries

TO DECORATE

g/½ oz toasted flaked almonds

tsp icing sugar

METHOD

Preheat the oven to 220°C/425°F/Gas Mark 7. ghtly grease a 35 x 25-cm/14 x 10-inch Swiss ll tin and line with baking parchment.

Place the eggs in a mixing bowl with the aster sugar. Place the bowl over a pan of hot ater and whisk until pale and thick.

3 Remove the bowl from the pan. Sift the flour and fold into the eggs. Add the hot water. Pour the mixture into the tin and bake for 8–10 minutes, until golden and set.

4 Turn the cake out on to a sheet of baking parchment. Peel off the lining paper and roll up the sponge tightly, along with the baking parchment. Wrap in a tea towel and set aside to cool.

5 To make the filling, mix together the fromage frais and the almond essence. Reserving a few strawberries for decoration, wash, hull and slice the remainder. Leave the mixture to chill in the refrigerator until required.

6 Unroll the sponge, spread the fromage frais mixture over it and sprinkle with strawberries. Roll up the sponge again and transfer to a serving plate. Sprinkle with almonds and dust lightly with icing sugar. Decorate with the reserved strawberries.

INDEX

B

baked apple & golden
    raisin dessert 28
berry cheesecake 30
bowls 10
buttery lemon tart 26

C

cake-baking 6, 8
chocolate 7, 9
    chocolate & pear
        cake 7, 25
    chocolate topping 12
classic carrot cake 7, 14
cookie sheets 11
cooling racks 11
cranberry & almond tart 11

D

dough 11

E

equipment 10–11

G

golden fruit cake 7, 16
golden raisin & cherry
    biscuits 7, 16

L

lemon
    cream butterflies 24
    sponge cake 15

M

measuring 8, 10
mini meringues 20
mixed fruit
    crumble 23
    pavlova 7, 21
mixing 8, 10
molasses biscuits 7, 27

P

pans 8, 11

R

raspberry & cream
    shortbread 7, 28
rolling pins 11
rules 8–9

S

sandwich cake &
    chocolate topping 12
scales 10
spatulas 8, 11

spices
    apple gingerbread 7, 2.
    bread & butter
        dessert 13
    fruit loaf 7, 17
storage 6
strainers 10
strawberry roulade 31

T

tarts 8–9, 11
treacle scones 27

W

wooden spoons 10